GROWING UP

FROM CHILD TO ADULT

ANITA GANERI

PETER BEDRICK BOOKS

NEW YORK

INTRODUCTION

In each of the world's six major religions, the most important times in a person's life are marked by special ceremonies. These are a bit like signposts on the journey through life, guiding a person from one stage of their life to the next. They also give people the chance to share their beliefs and their joys or sorrows, whether in celebrating a baby's birth, the change from child to adult, a wedding, or marking and remembering a person's death. For each occasion, there are prayers to be said, presents to give and receive, festive food to eat and stories to tell. Customs and ceremonies vary in different parts of the world. This book looks at just some of them.

GROWING UP

This book examines how people from the Hindu, Buddhist, Sikh, Jewish, Christian and Muslim faiths mark the beginning of adult life. This is often seen as a 'new life' when you make a firm commitment to your religion, learn more about it and start to take greater responsibility for your own actions.

In this book dates are written with BCE and CE, instead of BC and AD which are based on the Christian calendar. BCE means 'Before the Common Era' and it replaces BC (Before Christ). CE means 'in the Common Era' and it replaces AD (Anno Domini 'in the year of our Lord').

 This is the Hindu sacred symbol 'Om'. It expresses all the secrets of the universe.

 This wheel is a Buddhist symbol. Its eight spokes stand for eight points of the Buddha's teaching.

 This Sikh symbol is called the 'Ik onkar'. It means: 'There is only one God'.

 The Star of David is a Jewish symbol. It appears on the flag of Israel.

 The cross is a Christian symbol. It reminds Christians of how Jesus died on a cross.

 The star and crescent moon are symbols of Islam.

CONTENTS

A SACRED THREAD

When a Hindu boy is about ten years old, a very special ceremony takes place. This is called the Upanayana Samskara, or the rite of the sacred thread. It marks a new stage in the boy's life when he leaves his childhood behind. A priest studies the boy's horoscope, which was drawn up at his birth, to choose a lucky day for the ceremony. Girls do not have an Upanayana ceremony.

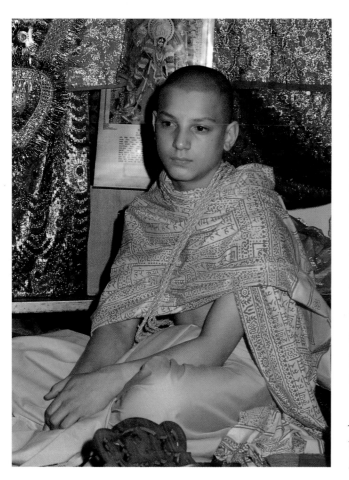

Getting ready

The Upanayana ceremony takes place at the boy's home or in the mandir (temple). Invitations are sent out to family and friends, and to ten Brahmins (priests). On the day itself the boy bathes and his head is completely shaved, apart from a small tuft at the back. Then he puts on new, clean clothes.

The sacred thread

The ceremony takes place in front of a sacred fire. Prayers are said to Agni, the god of fire, and butter is scattered in the flames. Then the priest sprinkles the sacred thread with water, and loops it over the boy's left shoulder and

A Hindu boy at his Upanayana ceremony. It is a very important time in his life. He is now ready to be counted as an adult.

The priest loops the sacred thread over the boy's left shoulder and under his right arm.

Praising the Sun

During the Upanayana Samskara ceremony the priests recite a hymn, called the 'Gayatri Mantra'. It comes from the *Rig Veda*, one of the holiest Hindu books:
'Let us meditate on the glory and brilliance of the Sun god, which lights up the Earth and heavens. May he inspire us and bless us.'

Afterwards, the boy kneels in front of his father and is taught the words of the hymn.

The three great Hindu gods – Brahma, Vishnu and Shiva

under his right arm. The thread is made of cotton, in two links. Each link has three threads and each thread has three strands. The strands represent the three most important Hindu gods – Brahma the creator, Vishnu the protector, and Shiva the destroyer. The boy must wear the thread throughout his life.

more than 2000 years ago. The rules include not eating meat, not gambling, not lying, and not harming any living creatures. In the past, a boy left home to live with a guru, or religious teacher, while he completed his studies. Today, he stays at home and enjoys a celebratory feast with his friends and family.

Boys arriving for their Upanayana ceremony. After the ceremony, boys used to leave their family home to live with their guru. Although this does not happen today, the boys still carry water pots and white bundles on sticks throughout the ceremony. The bundles contain food for the journey they would once have made.

Making promises

The sacred thread ceremony marks not only the start of a Hindu boy's adult life but also of his religious education. He promises to study the sacred books of Hinduism and to follow certain rules. These rules are called the Laws of Manu. They are named after a wise teacher and they were written

Four stages of life

Traditionally, an adult Hindu's life is divided into four stages, called ashramas. Each stage has its own special duties:

1. **Brahmacharya** Life as a student – begins with the sacred thread ceremony
2. **Grihastha** Married and working life
3. **Vanaprastha** Retirement
4. **Sannyasa** Life as a wandering holy man. The fourth stage is optional and few people enter it.

Holy books

The oldest Hindu sacred books are called the *Vedas*. They contain hymns, prayers and magic spells, more than 3500 years old. The holiest is the *Rig Veda*, or the 'Song of Knowledge'. It is a collection of 1028 hymns in praise of the gods. Other scriptures, called the *Upanishads*, talk about people's relationship with God. They were composed in about 800 BCE, and they are in the form of lessons between gurus and their pupils.

A holy man reads the Hindu sacred texts. At first these texts were memorised and passed on by word of mouth. Later they were written down in Sanskrit, the sacred Indian language.

The vanishing salt

This story comes from the *Chandogya Upanishad*.

A father was teaching his son about Brahman (God). He gave him some salt and told him to sprinkle it in a bowl of water. Then he told his son to take the salt out again. But this was impossible because the salt had dissolved.

"Take a sip of the water," the father said. The water tasted of salt.

"My son," said the father. "You cannot see it but the salt is still there. It is present in everything just like Brahman."

THE THREE JEWELS

Buddhists do not have a formal ceremony to welcome them into their faith. They simply recite the Three Jewels (see page 11). However, a special ceremony is held for boys entering a monastery to train as monks. This is called an ordination ceremony.

Becoming a monk

Some Buddhists leave their homes and possessions behind and devote their lives to studying and teaching the Buddha's message. They enter the sangha (community) of monks and nuns. Monks are known as bhikkhus, nuns are called bhikkhuni. In some Buddhist countries, young boys often spend a short time in a monastery as part of their education. They have their ordination ceremony when they are ten years old. Then they are called novice monks.

In Myanmar, boys set off for a monastery dressed in bright silk and riding on a horse. This is to imitate Siddhartha Gautama before he became the Buddha. He was a royal prince who gave up a life of luxury to become a monk.

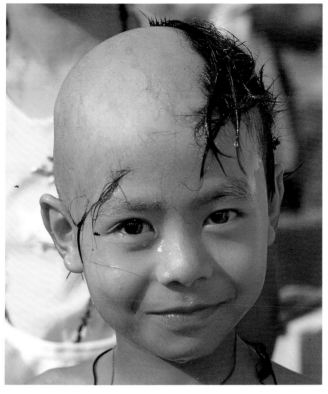

The Three Jewels

Becoming a Buddhist means making a commitment to the Three Jewels of Buddhism. These are the Buddha, the dharma (his teaching) and the sangha (the Buddhist community). They are called jewels because they are so precious:

'I go to the Buddha for refuge.
I go to the dharma for refuge.
I go to the sangha for refuge.'

A boy monk has his hair shaved off.

A boy is dressed in his monk's robes

A special ceremony

Before his ordination ceremony, a boy has his head shaved to show that he is not vain or concerned with worldly ties. Then he puts on a saffron (orange) or maroon robe. The very first Buddhist monks wore saffron robes because they harmonised with the colours of nature. During the ceremony, the boy recites the Three Jewels (see box) and promises to obey the Ten Precepts (see page 12).

Buddhist monks have very few possessions. *Everything the monks need is donated by well-wishers. These monks have been given food to put in their alms bowls.*

The Ten Precepts

Buddhist monks and nuns promise to obey ten rules of behaviour, called the Ten Precepts (Promises). These are:
1. Not harming living things
2. Not stealing
3. No sexual misconduct
4. Not telling lies
5. Not drinking alcohol or taking drugs
6. Not eating after midday, or too much
7. Not dancing or singing in a frivolous way
8. Not wearing jewellery or perfume
9. Not sleeping in a soft bed
10. Not taking gifts of money

All Buddhists follow the first five Precepts in their daily lives.

Life as a monk

Buddhist monks live strict, simple lives, reading and chanting from the sacred texts and meditating. They also look after the daily running of the monastery. Some work as teachers or help in the community. Traditionally, monks are only allowed to own eight items – three robes, an alms bowl, a belt, a razor, a water-strainer and a sewing needle. Young monks spend their time learning about the Buddha's teachings. They have to study hard. To become a fully ordained monk, a boy must wait until he is at least 20 years old.

Learning to read and chant the sacred texts

The first monks

The Buddha himself spent most of his life as a monk, travelling and teaching. One of his unlikeliest followers was an infamous robber, called Angoulimala. This terrible name means 'finger necklace' – for Angoulimala used to cut off his victims' fingers and wear them in a chain around his neck.

One day, Angoulimala saw the Buddha and started to chase him. But he just couldn't catch him, no matter how fast he ran.

"Stand still!" he shouted.

"I am still," said the Buddha. "You're the one who is moving."

Then the Buddha explained. Although his legs were moving, the Buddha's mind was calm and still. Angoulimala's mind, however, was racing with evil.

The Buddha's words touched the last bit of goodness left in the robber. He fell to his knees and begged the Buddha to make him a monk so that he could find stillness too.

JOINING THE KHALSA

For young Sikh boys and girls, entering the Sikh Khalsa, or family, is an important part of growing up and becoming full members of their faith. Many Sikhs enter when they are between 12 and 16 years old. But Sikhs can join the Khalsa at any age.

How the Khalsa began

In 1699, Guru Gobind Singh called all the Sikhs together. He asked if any of them were willing to die for their beliefs. At first, no one answered. Then one man stepped forward. Guru Gobind Singh took the man into his tent. When the Guru came out again, his sword was stained with blood. He asked the question again. Another man stepped forward. This happened five times. The crowd were frightened – had the Guru gone mad and killed the men? Then the Guru called the five men to come out, all alive and well. They became the Panj Piare, the beloved ones, the first members of the Khalsa.

Guru Gobind Singh and his wife, preparing a bowl of amrit (see page 15). Behind them stand the Panj Piare, the first five members of the Khalsa.

Amrit ceremony

A special ceremony is held in the gurdwara for Sikhs joining the Khalsa. It is led by five people who represent the Panj Piare, the first members of the Khalsa. Before the ceremony, the people who are to enter the Khalsa must bathe, wash their hair and put on clean clothes. They must also wear the Five Ks (see box). During the ceremony, they kneel on their right knee and drink some amrit, a mixture of sugar and water, from a large steel bowl. More amrit is sprinkled on their hair and eyes. After the ceremony everyone shares a bowl of karah parshad, a sweet made from flour, sugar and butter. This is to show that they are all equal.

The amrit ceremony in a gurdwara. The five men dressed in orange tunics represent the Panj Piare. The other people are joining the Khalsa. It is a very special day in their lives.

The five Ks

All Sikhs who become members of the Khalsa must promise to wear five things, set down by Guru Gobind Singh. Each begins with the letter 'K' in the Punjabi language.

1. Kesh – long hair. This shows devotion to God. Sikhs should not cut their hair but must keep it clean and tidy.
2. Kanga – a small wooden comb. It keeps the hair tidy. It reminds Sikhs how important it is to be well organised in daily life.
3. Kara – a steel bracelet. It is worn on the right wrist to show unity with God and the Khalsa. It reminds Sikhs that they must be strong, like steel, and stand up for what they believe.
4. Kirpan – a sword. This shows willingness to fight for justice. It must never be used for attacking people.
5. Kaccha – cotton shorts, worn today as underwear. In the past, Sikhs wore them for work. Shorts were more practical than the long, loose trousers that were usually worn.

A Sikh man wearing the five Ks

A turban is made of a piece of cloth fifteen feet long which is wound around the head.

Equal in name

When they enter the Khalsa, all Sikh men take the name 'Singh' which means lion and represents courage. They use it as a second name or as a surname. All Sikh women take the name 'Kaur' which means princess. They often use it as a second name between their first name and their family name. Sharing a name is a way of showing that they are all part of the same family.

Tying a turban

Sikhs wear a turban as a special sign of their faith. They are taught that the Gurus all wore turbans. A turban also helps to keep their long hair tidy (see page 15). Boys learn to tie a turban when they are about ten years old, at a turban-tying ceremony. Friends and relations come to watch and give the boy gifts of money to mark the happy occasion. Girls need not wear a turban. They cover their head and shoulders with a long scarf, often called a dupatta.

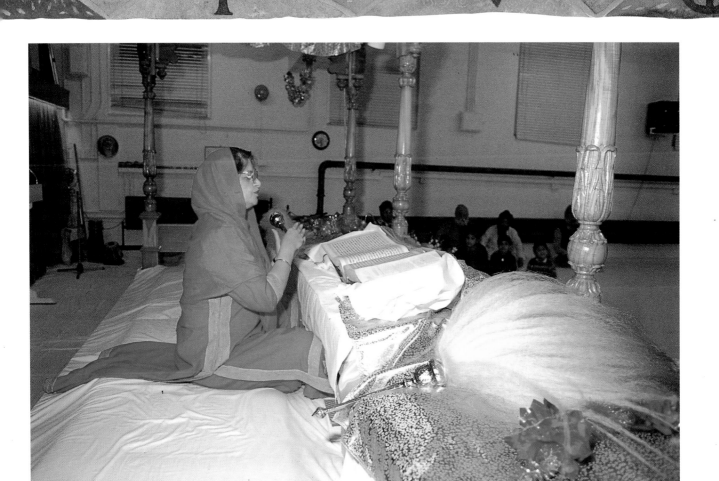

A Sikh woman reading from the Guru Granth Sahib, *the Sikh holy book. The* Guru Granth Sahib *is used in all Sikh worship. Inside the gurdwara it is placed on a throne, called a takht, as a sign of respect.*

Living as a Sikh

After the amrit ceremony, Sikhs are expected to live according to the rules of their religion. They pray every day and follow the teachings of the Gurus. They also promise to learn more about their religion and to read the *Guru Granth Sahib*, the Sikh holy book.

The Japji

Many prayers and hymns are recited during the amrit ceremony. This is part of the Japji hymn of Guru Nanak, who founded the Sikh religion:

'If your hands and feet are dusty, you wash them.
Likewise you wash dirty clothes.
But if your mind is filled with evil
It can only be cleaned by loving God's name.'

Obeying the Commandments

In the Jewish religion, boys have a ceremony to mark the start of their adult religious life. It is called a Bar Mitzvah and takes place when they are 13 years old. Some Jewish girls have a Bat Mitzvah when they are 12. These ceremonies show that they are old enough to understand and obey the Ten Commandments, the most important rules for Jews to follow.

Bar Mitzvah

Bar Mitzvah means 'a son of the commandment'. The ceremony takes place in the synagogue on the Shabbat (Saturday) after a boy's thirteenth birthday. Boys have to study hard for their Bar Mitzvah. They attend special classes in the synagogue to learn the rules and history of Judaism from the rabbi. They also learn the ancient Hebrew language so that they can read from the *Torah* (see page 20).

A Jewish boy at his Bar Mitzvah. He is reading a passage from the Torah. *He has rehearsed this moment many times! He uses a silver pointer, called a yad, to follow the words because the scrolls are too precious to touch.*

The ceremony

As the synagogue fills with worshippers, the boy waits near the bimah. This is a raised desk where the *Torah* is read. Then the service begins. The sacred scrolls of the *Torah* are taken from the Ark and placed on the bimah. The boy's big moment has arrived! He begins to read the passage he has learned. When he has finished, the rabbi says a blessing and reminds the boy of his duties and promises. Then the boy recites, in Hebrew, the special Bar Mitzvah prayer. Afterwards, there is a meal to celebrate the happy occasion and the boy is given gifts, cards and good wishes!

Dressed for prayer

At his Bar Mitzvah a boy wears his tallit, a prayer shawl, for the first time. This shows that he is now an adult. He can also wear tefillin bound to his arm opposite his heart, and on his forehead. These are two small black leather boxes. Inside are tiny scrolls with passages from the *Torah*. On his head he wears a kippah, or cap.

A Bar Mitzvah in Jerusalem. These boys are carrying the sacred Torah scrolls.

A boy wearing a kippah, tallit and tefillin

A selection of cards for Bar Mitzvah and Bat Mitzvah. There are many designs to choose from.

Special duties

Now that the boy is Bar Mitzvah, he is responsible for religious duties. He can take part in synagogue services and be counted as one of the ten men who must usually be present before a service can begin.

The Torah

The Torah *scrolls*

The *Torah*, or Books of Teaching, are the most important Jewish holy books. They are believed to have been given to Moses by God on Mount Sinai. Copies are handwritten, in Hebrew, on scrolls. In the synagogue, the scrolls are wrapped in embroidered silk or velvet cloths, called mantles, and kept in an alcove, called the Ark (left). They are placed on the bimah for reading. The books of the *Torah* contain stories about the creation of the world, the first Jews and the rules by which a Jew should live.

Bat Mitzvah

Bat Mitzvah means 'a daughter of the commandments'. A Bat Mitzvah ceremony is held on a Sunday, at the end of a service. Girls stand before the congregation and recite one of the Psalms. Then each girl reads the story of a great Jewish woman from the scriptures. After this, the girls say the Shema prayer (see box) and repeat the Ten Commandments. The rabbi blesses them and talks to them about their future lives and responsibilities. Then everyone joins in the congratulations.

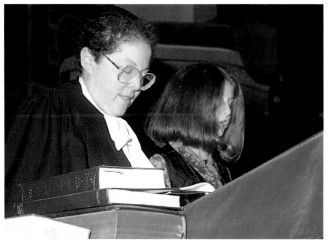

A girl practising for her Bat Mitzvah in the synagogue. She wants to be word perfect. Next to her is the rabbi.

Shema prayer

The Shema is the most important Jewish prayer. It sums up what the Jews believe and reminds them to love and worship God. This is how the Shema begins:

'Hear, O Israel,
The Lord is our God. The Lord is One.
Love the Lord your God with all your heart,
And with all your soul,
And with all your might.'

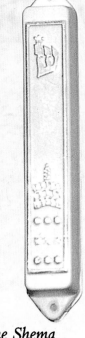

The case (right) and tiny scroll (left) are called a mezuzah. The scroll has part of the Shema written on it. It is rolled up, put in the case and fixed to the doorpost of a Jewish home. Jews touch it as they go in and out, as a sign of respect.

CONFIRMING YOUR FAITH

In the Christian faith, ceremonies are held to mark the beginning of a person's 'new life' in the Church. Different branches of the Church have different ways of celebrating this important time.

Being confirmed

In the Anglican and Roman Catholic Churches, a Confirmation service is held for young people or for adults of any age who wish to become church members. Confirmation means making something firmer or stronger. In this case, people confirm their Christian beliefs and promise to follow the teachings of Jesus Christ. Before the ceremony, they learn more about what it means to be a Christian at classes held in their local church. Other Christian Churches hold similar services to welcome people into full membership of their church.

This is a special day for these girls when they will take part in Communion (see page 24) for the first time. They wear white to mark the occasion.

(see page 24)

The ceremony

The Confirmation ceremony is carried out by a bishop. First he talks about the promises the Confirmation candidates will make. Then he asks each of them:

"Do you turn to Christ? Do you repent of your sins? Do you renounce evil?"

They reply: "I turn to Christ. I repent of my sins. I renounce evil."

Then the candidates kneel before the bishop. He lays his hands on their heads and says: "Confirm, O Lord, your servant, with your Holy Spirit."

The person is now counted as a full member of the church and takes part in Holy Communion (see page 24).

Adult baptism

Baptism is another service that marks a person's commitment to the Christian Church. Many Christians are baptised as babies but they can be baptised at any age. In the Baptist Church, people wait until they are in their teens or even older. Then they stand in a pool set in the floor of the church and are dipped right under the water as they make their promises.

A baptism service for adults. The person in the pool is totally immersed under the water.

Jesus is baptised

When he was about 30 years old, Jesus was baptised by his cousin, John, in the River Jordan. When Jesus stepped out of the water, a white dove flew down from the sky and settled on his shoulder. This was a symbol of the Holy Spirit, sent by God. Then God's voice was heard, saying;

"This is my beloved Son, in whom I am well pleased."

After this, Jesus began his new life of teaching and healing.

Holy Communion

As full members of the Church, the people who have been baptised or confirmed take part in a special ceremony, called Holy Communion. During Communion, they eat a small piece of bread and drink a sip of wine. Both the bread and the wine have been blessed by the priest. For Christians, the bread represents Jesus's body and the wine represents his blood. In this way, Christians remember and give thanks for Jesus's life and death. Holy Communion is also called the Eucharist which means 'thanksgiving', the Mass, the Divine Liturgy or the Breaking of the Bread.

A priest blessing the Communion bread and wine. The tall goblets contain wine. The bowls contain small round wafers of bread. These have a cross imprinted on them.

The last supper

Holy Communion reminds Christians of the last meal Jesus shared with his disciples on the day before he died. This is called the Last Supper.

Jesus and his disciples sat at a long table on which a meal of bread, meat and wine was laid. The disciples' mood was very solemn. They knew something was wrong. Jesus picked up the bread, blessed it and broke it into pieces. He gave a piece to each disciple.

"Eat this bread," he said. "It is my body."

Then he passed a cup of wine to each of them in turn.

"Drink this wine," he said. " It is my blood."

Jesus knew he was going to die. He told his friends to remember him whenever they ate bread or drank wine. This is what Christians still do today.

This stained glass window in a church shows Jesus and his disciples at the Last Supper.

FIVE PILLARS OF FAITH

As young children Muslims start to learn about Islam, including how to pray and behave in a mosque. By the age of 12 or 13, they are expected to take on the duties of adult Muslims.

The words of the Shahadah, written in Arabic, above the doorway of a mosque

The Five Pillars

The five main duties for Muslims are called the Five Pillars of Islam. They are called 'pillars' because they help to support Islam, just as real pillars support a building. They are:

1. Shahadah, or the statement of faith. It says that 'There is no other God but Allah, and Muhammad is his prophet.'
2. Salah, or prayer. Muslims must pray five times a day, at set times, facing in the direction of the city of Mecca.
3. Zakah, or giving money to the poor.
4. Sawm, or fasting. Muslims do not eat or drink from dawn until sunset during the Islamic month of Ramadan.
5. Hajj, or pilgrimage. Muslims try to make a pilgrimage to Mecca at least once in their lives.

Muslims at the Ka'bah shrine in Mecca during the Hajj pilgrimage.

The Night of Power

On the Night of Power (Laylat ul-Qadr), during the month of Ramadan, Muslims remember the night on which Muhammad received the *Qur'an*. Muhammad was sleeping in a cave on Mount Hira, near Mecca, where he had gone to pray and meditate. Suddenly the Archangel Jibril appeared before him and began to tell him the words now known as the *Qur'an*. Muhammad could not read or write. He memorised the words by reciting them. Later, he received further messages and eventually his followers wrote them down and collected them together as a book.

Learning to read the Qur'an *at a mosque school*

Reading the Qur'an

When they are about seven years old, Muslim children go to a mosque school. There they learn to read the *Qur'an* which is written in Arabic. The *Qur'an* is the Muslims' holy book. Muslims believe that every word of the *Qur'an* comes from Allah. It contains Allah's guidance about how people should live. The *Qur'an* was given to the prophet Muhammad and can never be changed. Copies of the *Qur'an* are treated with great respect. Some Muslims learn the whole *Qur'an* by heart.

Fact files

Hinduism

- **Numbers of Hindus:** *c.*732 million
- **Where began:** India (*c.* 2500 BCE)
- **Founder figure:** None
- **Major deities:** Thousands of gods and goddesses representing different aspects of Brahman, the great soul. The three most important gods are Brahma the creator, Vishnu the protector, and Shiva the destroyer.
- **Places of worship:** Mandirs (temples), shrines
- **Holy books:** *Vedas, Upanishads, Ramayana, Mahabharata*

Buddhism

- **Numbers of Buddhists:** *c.* 314 million
- **Where began:** Nepal/India (6th century BCE)
- **Founder figure:** Siddhartha Gautama, who became known as the Buddha
- **Major deities:** None, the Buddha did not want people to worship him as a god.
- **Places of worship:** Viharas (monasteries or temples), stupas (shrines)
- **Holy books:** *Tripitaka* (*Pali Canon*), *Diamond Sutra* and many others

Sikhism

- **Numbers of Sikhs:** *c.* 18 million
- **Where began:** India (15th century CE)
- **Founder figure:** Guru Nanak
- **Major deities:** One God whose word was brought to people by ten earthly gurus, or teachers.
- **Places of worship:** Gurdwaras (temples)
- **Holy book:** *Guru Granth Sahib*

Judaism

- **Number of Jews:** *c.* 17 million
- **Where began:** Middle East (*c.* 2000 BCE)
- **Important figures:** Abraham, Moses, Isaac, Jacob
- **Major deities:** One God who created and rules over the world.
- **Places of worship:** Synagogues
- **Holy books:** *Tenakh* (Hebrew *Bible*), *Torah* (the first five books of the *Tenakh*), *Talmud*

Christianity

- **Numbers of Christians:** *c.* 2000 million
- **Where began:** Middle East (1st century CE)
- **Important figure:** Jesus Christ
- **Major deities:** One God, in three aspects – as the Father (creator of the world), as the Son (Jesus Christ), and as the Holy Spirit
- **Places of worship:** Churches, cathedrals, chapels
- **Holy books:** *Bible* (Old and New Testaments)

Islam

- **Numbers of Muslims:** *c.* 1000 million
- **Where began:** Saudi Arabia (*c.* 610 CE)
- **Important figure:** The prophet, Muhammad
- **Major deities:** One God, Allah, who revealed his wishes to the prophet Muhammad.
- **Places of worship:** Mosques
- **Holy books:** The *Qur'an*

GLOSSARY

amrit A special mixture of sugar and water used at Sikh ceremonies.

ashrama One of four stages in a Hindu's life.

baptism A ceremony at which a person becomes a full member of the Christian Church. They are sprinkled or bathed in water as a sign that they are cleansed from sin.

Bar Mitzvah A ceremony which marks the start of a Jewish boy's responsibility for religious duties.

Bat Mitzvah A ceremony which marks the start of a Jewish girl's responsibility for religious duties.

bhikkhu A Buddhist monk.

bhikkhuni A Buddhist nun.

bimah A raised desk in the front of a synagogue. The *Torah* scrolls are placed here for reading.

Brahmin A member of the highest caste (group) in Hindu society. This is the group from which Hindu priests come.

Confirmation A special service held for young people and adults who wish to confirm their membership of the Christian Church.

dharma An ancient Indian word meaning law. In Buddhism, it means the Buddha's teachings.

disciple A person who follows a religious leader.

dupatta A long scarf worn by Sikh women.

guru A Sikh or Hindu religious teacher or leader.

Hajj The pilgrimage to Mecca which all Muslims try to make at least once in their lives. This is one of the Five Pillars of Islam.

karah parshad A sweet food shared out at Sikh ceremonies.

Khalsa The name given to the group of Sikhs who have become full members of their faith. The word Khalsa means 'the pure ones'.

kippah A head covering worn by a Jewish boy or man.

mandir A Hindu place of worship, temple.

Panj Piare The first five members of the Sikh Khalsa. The words mean the 'five beloved ones'.

rabbi A Jewish religious teacher who leads the worship in a synagogue.

Ramadan The Muslim month of fasting.

Rig Veda One of the oldest and holiest Hindu sacred books. There are three other *Vedas*.

Salah Muslim prayers. Muslims must pray five times a day. This is one of the Five Pillars of Islam.

samskara A ceremony which marks a special time in a Hindu's life. There are 16 in total.

sangha The community of Buddhists.

Sanskrit An ancient Indian language. The Hindu sacred books are written in Sanskrit.

Sawm For Muslims, this means fasting between dawn and sunset during Ramadan. This is one of the Five Pillars of Islam.

Shahadah A statement of Muslim belief, that there is only one God and Muhammad is his prophet. This is one of the Five Pillars of Islam.

Shema An important Jewish prayer which reminds Jews to love and worship God.

tallit A prayer shawl worn by Jewish boys or men.

tefillin Two small leather boxes worn by Jewish boys or men. Inside are tiny scrolls on which are written passages from the *Torah*.

Torah Jewish teaching; the first five books of the Hebrew *Bible*.

Upanishads Holy books of the Hindus

Zakah For Muslims, this means giving money to the poor. This is one of the Five Pillars of Islam.

INDEX